A Certain

Roughness

in Their Syntax

PREVIOUS VOLUMES: TUPELO PRESS POETRY IN TRANSLATION

Abiding Places: Korea, South and North, by Ko Un
Translated from Korean by Hillel Schwartz and Sunny Jung

Invitation to a Secret Feast: Selected Poems, by Joumana Haddad
Translated from Arabic by Khaled Mattawa with Najib Awad, Issa Boullata,
    Marilyn Hacker, Joumana Haddad, Henry Matthews, and David Harsent

Night, Fish and Charlie Parker, by Phan Nhien Hao
Translated from Vietnamese by Linh Dinh

Stone Lyre: Poems of René Char
Translated from French by Nancy Naomi Carlson

This Lamentable City: Poems of Polina Barskova
Edited by Ilya Kaminsky and translated from Russian by the editor with Katie
    Farris, Rachel Galvin, and Matthew Zapruder

New Cathay: Contemporary Chinese Poetry
Edited by Ming Di and translated from Chinese by the editor with Neil Aitken,
    Katie Farris, Christopher Lupke, Tony Barnstone, Nick Admussen, Jonathan
    Stalling, Afaa M. Weaver, Eleanor Goodman, Ao Wang, Dian Li, Kerry Shawn
    Keys, Jennifer Kronovet, Elizabeth Reitzell, and Cody Reese

Ex-Voto, by Adélia Prado
Translated from Brazilian Portuguese by Ellen Doré Watson

Gossip and Metaphysics: Russian Modernist Poems and Prose
Edited by Katie Farris, Ilya Kaminsky, and Valzhyna Mort, with translations by
    the editors and others

Calazaza's Delicious Dereliction, by Suzanne Dracius
Translated from French by Nancy Naomi Carlson

Canto General: Song of the Americas, by Pablo Neruda
Translated from Spanish by Mariela Griffor and Jeffrey Levine

Hammer with No Master, by René Char
Translated from French by Nancy Naomi Carlson

Bailando en Odesa, Spanish-language edition of Ilya Kaminsky's *Dancing in
    Odessa*
Translated by Mariela Griffor

A Certain Roughness in Their Syntax

Poems by

JORGE AULICINO

Translated by JUDITH FILC

TUPELO PRESS
North Adams, Massachusetts

A Certain Roughness in Their Syntax.
Translation and introduction copyright © 2017 Judith Filc.
All rights reserved.

Library of Congress Cataloging-in-Publication Data
Names: Aulicino, Jorge Ricardo, 1949- author. | Filc, Judith, translator.
Title: A certain roughness in their syntax / Jorge Aulicino ; poems
translated by Judith Filc. Other titles: Cierta dureza en la sintaxis.
English | Tupelo Press poetry in translation.
Description: First edition. | North Adams, Massachusetts : Tupelo Press,
  2017. | Series: Tupelo Press poetry in translation
Identifiers: LCCN 2017043152 | ISBN 9781946482020 (pbk. original : alk.
paper) Classification: LCC PQ7798.1.U45 C5413 2017 | DDC 861/.64--
dc23

Cover and text designed and composed in Adobe Minion by Dede Cummings.
Special thanks to Laura Cesarco Eglin for editorial assistance.
Cover art: "Gawet's Debris #2" by Don Ross (http://donrossphotography.com).
Used with permission of the artist.

First edition: December 2017.

TUPELO PRESS
P.O. Box 1767, NORTH ADAMS, MASSACHUSETTS 01247
(413) 664–9611 / editor@tupelopress.org / www.tupelopress.org

Tupelo Press is an award-winning independent literary press that publishes
fine fiction, nonfiction, and poetry in books that are a joy to hold as well
as read. Tupelo Press is a registered 501(c)(3) nonprofit organization,
and we rely on public support to carry out our mission of publishing
extraordinary work that may be outside the realm of the large commercial
publishers. Financial donations are welcome and are tax deductible.

Produced with support from the National Endowment for the Arts

ART WORKS.
arts.gov

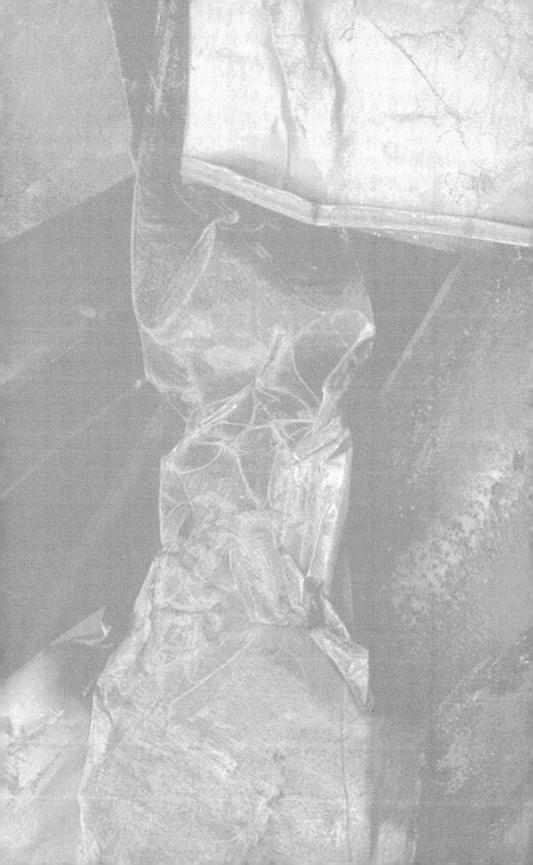

Contents

Translator's Introduction

WHEN ASKED WHY HE WRITES, Jorge Aulicino answers that he started writing poetry because he was fascinated by the movements of words in a poem; there, "words behaved differently." He is particularly interested in images, and believes that poetic images are "physical images,"[1] — visual objects seen with the eyes of the mind. The object, he says, "is charged with imagination and spirit, and there is no object that is not charged also with history, with life, with humanity." When he writes a poem, he tries to "imagine it materially," even if the poem will finally become an abstract idea, a meditation.[2]

His point of departure, he says, is always what he sees. In the first poem of Book First of *La línea del coyote* [The Line of the Coyote] (1999), he talks about "the traces of an excavator in the rain / seen in passing out the window," and asks, "Don't you think that the essence of things is abandonment by a god?" That is why painting plays a key role in his poetry, and many of his poems talk about painting and painters — Caravaggio, Bacon, Cézanne. "What appeals to me is the framing and freezing; stopping there to see every detail. A kind of obsession for details." In "La poesía era un bello país" ["Poetry was a beautiful country"], from *La caída de los cuerpos* [Falling Bodies] (1983), poetry is "what water doesn't take away what stays in the sink / spinning refusing resisting / shell from an egg potato peelings."

Aulicino started writing and publishing poetry at a young age, along with his career as a journalist. He worked for a variety of publications for almost fifty years, and retired recently. He believes that journalistic writing had a positive influence on his poetry; it taught him to organize information and ideas. He learned from his first boss that a good journalistic text ought to be "brief, precise, potent." There was magic in that style, says Aulicino. "I felt that the magic of language, the function of revealing, of making things alive and visible, could be found in that prose." Journalism, he adds, "taught me economy. And it taught me to narrate more effectively in poetry." The worlds of poetry and journalism communicated and "coexisted comfortably."[3]

Aulicino is one of Argentina's most renowned and influential living poets. In 2015 he received Argentina's National Poetry Award. Literary historians divide poetry movements in Argentina since the 1920s into ten-year categories called "generations," and critics consider Aulicino to be part of the so-called 1970s generation. So far, there have been nine generations of poets, starting with the 1920s avant-garde, which represents the second break with tradition after Spanish-American *Modernismo* in the 1890s. The third big break took place in the 1960s, with the introduction of the language of pop culture and journalism into poetry and the centrality of political engagement in literature and the arts. Argentine 1960s poetry was playful, profane, abundant, and strongly political.

The poets of the 1970s were writing under very different conditions. Between 1976 and 1983, Argentines were the victims of a bloody dictatorship. Repression was fierce, and censorship rampant. Many poets suffered the consequences: they were killed, disappeared, or forced into exile. Writing was still political, but it became stark; poems were brief, and their language ascetic, as in "*Ed e subito sera*," a poem from Aulicino's third collection, *La caída de los cuerpos* (whose title is a quote from a very brief poem by Salvatore

Quasimodo): "And how strange is / the fall / of objects / in the light / And how strange / the corruption / of the objects // (in the light)."

Emphasis was placed on what was not said. In his poem on "Cézanne" in the same book, Aulicino writes:

Blank spaces in Cézanne's last paintings
tell the experts
that he had pushed his theory to the extreme.
(. . .)
Why didn't Cézanne want to paint what his eyes,
even when moving with his body from right to left,
from left to right, could not see?[4]

The Argentine 1970s poets, with their predilection for simple but carefully crafted language and their focus on the power of silence, marked my own poetry. I discovered Aulicino when I was twenty years old and had started taking poetry writing seriously. The first book of his I read was *La caída de los cuerpos*, published in 1983, when the dictatorship was ending. I was also reading books by other poets of that generation, among them Irene Gruss, Guillermo Boido, and Daniel Freidemberg. When I started translating Spanish-American poetry into English, with the aim of increasing its readership outside Latin America, Aulicino was first on my list.

In addition to his own writing, Aulicino has greatly contributed to the dissemination of poetry in the entire Spanish-speaking world in two different ways. Since 2006, he has administered a poetry blog, *Otra iglesia es imposible*, which has exceeded two million visits, offering its readers poetry from all over the world. Aulicino has also translated some of the greatest Italian poets into Spanish, including Dante, Pavese, Pasolini, Annedda, and Forti. His translation of *The Divine Comedy* quickly sold out and received high praise from the critics.

Aulicino defines two stages in his poetry. In the 1970s and 1980s, his poems were "brief, tied to specific circumstances, to historical constructions, but always as flashes, incomplete images." Then in the 1990s he started writing longer poems, connecting the fragments through a process of association. The first stage includes the following books: *Vuelo bajo* [Flying Low], *Poeta antiguo* [Ancient Poet], *La caída de los cuerpos* [Falling Bodies], *Paisaje con autor* [Landscape with Author], *Hombres en un restaurante* [Men in a Restaurant], and *Almas en movimiento* [Souls in Motion]. The second comprises *La línea del coyote* [The Line of the Coyote], *Las Vegas, La Nada* [Nothingness], *La luz checoslovaca* [Czech Light], *Hostias* [Hosts], *Máquina de faro* [Lighthouse Machine], *Ituzaingó*, *Primera Junta*, *Cierta dureza en la sintaxis* [*A Certain Roughness in Their Syntax*], *El capital* [Capital], *Libro del engaño y el desengaño* [The Book of Deceit and Disappointment], *El Cairo* [Cairo] and *Corredores en el parque* [Runners in the Park].

A Certain Roughness in Their Syntax, originally published in 2008, belongs to the second stage. It is a multilayered, multi-centered text where different registers and lyrical voices mingle and interact. In a complex web of striking images, Aulicino reflects on the history of the Western world and the rise and fall of its empires. The poems portray the thirst for gold, the proliferation of death, the uselessness of conquest, and a lack of concern for the downtrodden (those he has called elsewhere the "pariahs of the empire"); "troys, babylons, thebes, stables and markets / are incessantly built and demolished," he writes. The Spaniards found "no Eldorado. Only the waves and the dribble of the dead." In the final poem, Attila the Hun travels through a present-day city in a Porsche. With profound irony, Aulicino depicts a victorious conqueror who is actually a failure ("his quest is scenes of a poorly copied film"). Then we learn that Attila is all of us — his face "is that of the murderer in the papers, the rogue, the florist, or the incidental soccer hero."

This book also takes a different yet related direction, exploring the interconnection between subject and object. Images blend human beings and things, instilling life in matter. The stoplights are "bones of huge, steeped crustaceans." Buildings are "resigned to their perplexity." According to the great cosmogonies, "rocks are the bones of giants, / or men trickled from their open veins, / or the sea and the rivers are the remnants of their dissolution."

In a recent interview,[5] Aulicino referred to the presence of the medieval bestiary in the book: "Those ordinary animals endowed with strange properties (. . .), or the beings that are a fusion of two or three animals, gave me the impression that they represent our current human zoo; we are made of functions and parts that are utterly useless to the economy and to history. And we are also made of history."

I believe that the driving force of *A Certain Roughness in Their Syntax* is an inquiry into language and meaning in a variety of dimensions. One is the effect of colonization on language, the relationship between power and meaning: the colonizers "sought the faded clarity of things." Another dimension is the degradation of language that accompanies the decline of our civilization (buildings shift "toward the worn-out color of the words themselves — ghostly sounds"). There are also the consequences of war — the "frozen syntax of gunpowder." And I believe yet another (most important) dimension is the production of meaning in art. The question anxiously asked in the first poem, "What are you talking about? What are you talking about?" returns throughout the book under different guises. In Poem 10 the protagonist wonders "how to say: / how to say with the syntax of several hands / what was grasped by the painting, or what the painting / has built." In poem 12, Ezra the artist paints with a dry brush "the vivid color of what was alive." In poem 18, Bertolt "knew what it was about," but this certainty has been lost.

In these poems, world history and national history mingle with the poet's biography — his immigrant grandparents, his childhood neighborhood, the radically transforming events that occurred during his lifetime. There is a combination of the social and the personal, reflection and emotion that is supported by a web of apparently chaotic images. The quick succession of associations (what Aulicino has called "a flow of the mind") and the unexpected connections created by these images will infallibly move, disturb, or shake the reader: bodies strewn in the battle field; a sullen shack under a stormy night; vicious plants climbing the last cliffs; the nomad "surrounded by hawk and hippogriff, parcae and grapes."

The result is a deeply empathetic study of humankind. *A Certain Roughness in Their Syntax* is a major work by one of Argentina's best and most influential poets.

ENDNOTES

1. From an interview with Daniel Gigena for *La Nación* daily, December 14th, 2015.

2. From an interview with Augusto Munaro for *Los Andes* daily, March 27, 2010.

3. From an interview with Augusto Munaro for *Gramma* XXI (47), 2010.

4. The quotations are my own translations from poems in *Estación Finlandia: Poemas reunidos 1974–2011*, Buenos Aires: Bajo la luna, 2012.

5. op. cit., Munaro for *Gramma* XXI (47), 2010.

A Certain
Roughness
in Their Syntax

1

Cierta dureza en la sintaxis indicaba la poca versatilidad
de aquellos cadáveres; el betún cuarteado de las botas
y ese decir desligado del verbo; verbos auxiliares,
modos verbales elegantemente suspendidos, elididos,
en la sabia equitación de una vieja práctica.
¿De qué hablás, de qué hablás? Pero si fue ayer . . .
Fue ayer . . . Estabas frente al lago de ese río:
qué lejana esa costa, qué neblinosa y mañanera.
Lo tenías todo, no te habías arrastrado en la escoria
de las batallas perdidas antes de empezadas,
no andabas en el orín de estos muertos . . .
Lo comprendo, no era el Danubio, era el Paraná
que marea porque viene del cielo cerebral, pero aun así . . .
¿Se justifica la alegre inacción, el pensamiento venteado?
Abeja: la más pequeña de las aves, nace de la carne del buey.
Araña: gusano que se alimenta del aire. Calandria: la que
canta la enfermedad y puede curarla. Perdiz: ave embustera.

1

A certain roughness in their syntax signaled the lack of
versatility of the corpses; the cracked polish of the boots,
and that diction detached from the verb; auxiliary verbs,
elegantly suspended verbal moods
elided by the wise horsemanship of an old trade.
What are you talking about, what are you talking about?
But it was yesterday...Yesterday...You stood before the lake of
    that river:
How remote that shore, how hazy and early-bird.
You had it all; you hadn't crawled among the dregs of
battles lost before they started,
you didn't linger amid the urine of those dead...
I understand. It wasn't the Danube, it was the Parana,
bewildering in its descent from the cerebral skies, but even so...
Is the joyful inaction, the airy thought justified?
Bee: the smallest of birds, is born of ox meat.
Spider: worm that feeds on air. Lark: the one that
sings illnesses and can cure them. Partridge: lying bird.

2

Es buena esta ciudad. Podrías amarla. Cuando
el tictac de la ortografía, el trabajo incesante en la inflexión,
te permite respirar, la mirás. Lo saben tus vecinos:
salís al balcón en paños menores y mirás el perfil industrial
de la vereda de enfrente, orlado por fresnos secos,
el polvo aceitoso pegado a los flancos de la estrategia.

Mapas mohosos en los revoques de este mundo de tres lados.
Euclides derrotado.
El blanco mediterráneo,
al fin, con la historia que tan bien conoces; quiero decir,
los edificios de los 60 ahora antiguos, viran todos al pardo,
al color gastado de las mismas palabras, frases sobre frases
en los talleres mecánicos,
en la arquitectura demolida,
en los huecos zaguanes que dan a los fragmentos:
sonidos fantasmales. Sabemos adonde van los muertos,
pero ¿adónde van las voces?

Esta ciudad no deja de hacer ruido,
es el sonido
el que muele el pavimento.

2

This city is good. You might love it. When
the tick-tock of spelling, the ceaseless work on inflection
allows you to breathe, you look at her. Your neighbors know it.
You go out on the balcony in your underwear and look at the
    industrial profile of
the opposite sidewalk, trimmed with dry ash trees,
the oily dust stuck to the flanks of strategy.

Moldy maps in the plasters of this three-sided world.
Euclid defeated.
Mediterranean white,
finally, with the story you know so well. I mean,
the now-old 1960s buildings all veer toward brown,
toward the faded color of the same words, phrases upon phrases
in the repair shops,
in the bulldozed architecture,
in the hollow entrance halls that lead to fragments —
ghostly sounds. We know where the dead go but,
what of their voices?
This city does not stop making noises;
it is sound that
grinds the pavement.

3

Me dijiste la otra noche que las grandes cosmogonías
no tienen dioses creadores. Casi siempre el mundo
ha nacido de la propia destrucción de los primeros titanes.
Y esto es que las rocas son los huesos de un gigante
o que los hombres gotearon de sus venas abiertas
o que el mar y los ríos son lo que queda de su disolución.
En esta transformación de los grandiosos cadáveres
reina casi siempre una pandilla con la que conviene aliarse.
No entienden la plegaria. Hay que hablarles claro.
Sobre todo, nos ayudan o desgracian según sea
la simpatía espontánea que inspiramos en sus raras cabezas.
Y la tarde es un león embalsamado. Y los semáforos,
huesos de enormes crustáceos macerados.
Y Odín nos acompaña en estos campamentos oxidados.
Y Zeus mira de costado; el más obtuso y el más sabio.

3

Last night you told me that great cosmogonies have no
creator gods. The world has nearly always emerged from
the destruction of the first titans.
And thus rocks are the bones of giants,
or men trickled from their open veins,
or the sea and rivers are remnants of their dissolution.
In this transformation of magnificent corpses
a gang nearly always rules with which alliance is advisable.
They don't understand prayer. You must speak to them clearly.
Above all, they will help or ruin us based on the
spontaneous friendliness we arouse in their strange minds.
And the afternoon is an embalmed lion. And stoplights,
the bones of huge, steeped crustaceans.
And Odin is with us in these rusted camps.
And Zeus looks sideways — the most obtuse, and the wisest.

4

La comadreja representa a quienes estuvieron deseosos
de la palabra divina, pero que nada hacen con ella
cuando la han recibido. Y crían en las orejas.
La comadreja representa a quienes quisieron la gracia
y la gracia les fue dada, para nada.
No te muevas si encontrás a la comadreja
en la escalera o en el asiento de un taxi.
Reptará su pensamiento hacia lugares hollados,
porque, segura de la gracia y la palabra,
no se le ocurre qué hacer sino vagar
por donde hubo ciudades que los cjércitos
aplastaron con botas y llenaron de condones.
Más bien continuá construyendo el merecimiento
para que descienda la luz blanca o celeste sobre vos,
cuando realmente te distraigas en tu trabajo de desollar,
carpir, doblar, aventar, guardar o sacudir.
Aunque andes descalzo por los muelles ásperos
de tu propio pensamiento, habrás de distraerte profundamente
para no recibir en vano la amistad del reino,
para no deambular con la comadreja.

4

The weasel represents those who desired the
divine word but do nothing with it once
they have it. And they breed in their ears.
The weasel represents those who sought grace
and to whom grace was granted, for nothing.
Don't budge if you find the weasel on the
stairs or a cab seat.
Its thought will crawl into treaded places because,
certain about grace and words,
it can think of nothing to do but wander
where cities stood that armies
crushed with boots and filled with condoms.
Rather, keep accruing merit
so that the white or sky-blue light descends on you
when you're truly diverted from your skinning,
hoeing, folding, winnowing or shaking.
Even if you walk barefoot through the rough docks of your own
thoughts, your attention will be deeply diverted
so as not to accept in vain the kingdom's friendship,
so as not to roam with the weasel.

5

Es cierto que entre las aves medievales el árbol es libre.
Y aún hoy es libre entre la folletería de la abundancia.
Y es libre entre las piedras que suben y bajan a su alrededor.
Y libre entre las orlas de edificios que suben y bajan.
Y lo ves libre en los patios de los hospitales
y de los hospicios y tras los galpones y entre los techos.
A él va el gato. Astuto. Tenue. Y la musaraña va al árbol.
Y la hormiga. Y la tormenta y la luz que se esconde.
En el árbol hay trampas y gatos y botellas perdidas.
El árbol es amigo del bisel y de la penumbra.
Es más libre que el corsario.

El árbol
conserva la forma
tenuemente, sin rigidez.
Cada ciprés es un ciprés.
Y los miles de fresnos no son el fresno.
Si hubo dioses, amaron el árbol.
O combatieron por el árbol,
pero nunca gobernaron el árbol y nunca lo dijeron.

5

It is true that amid medieval birds, the tree is free.
And even now 'tis free amid the leaflets of abundance;
and free amid the stones going up and down around it;
and free amid the trims of buildings going up and down.
And you see it, free, in the courtyards of hospitals and
workhouses, and behind sheds and between roofs.
Toward it goes the cat. Cunning. Faint. And the shrew goes to the
    tree.
And the ant. And the storm, the hiding light.
On the tree there are traps and cats and lost bottles.
The tree is a friend of the bevel and the half-light.
It is freer than the corsairs.

The tree
preserves its shape
faintly, without stiffness.
Each cypress is a cypress.
And the thousands of ash trees are not the ash tree.
If gods existed once, they loved the tree.
Or fought for the tree,
yet never ruled over it or uttered it.

6

No diste baptisterio a la paz interior, y por un plazo
de difícil mensura pagarás en piezas de a cinco.

Todo el tiempo, mientras ibas de la misa a la armería
se sucedieron las operaciones bursátiles y anduvo
todo a su debida máquina, arrojando aceite
por las juntas, dando a cima el verso;
se llenaron de aguas de drenaje
las cuencas marítimas; trepidó el garaje,
se liquidaron honorarios; tuvieron
su tiempo el nacimiento, el crematorio.
¿A qué la prisa? Usa sabiamente el tiempo del pago.
Coloca vientre de sapo sobre el hematoma.
Siéntate en tu lugar, cala tus gafas, di que el arte
estatuario es simple y canta la verdad de los otros.
Te reconocerán por el carmesí de tus acentos.
Porque has usado verde y rosa, tilo y cortadera
para decir tu labia aprendida en el silencio.
Eres el que, débil y cansino, en el escudo lleva la hercinia,
ave cuyo plumaje produce efectos de luz en la sombra.
Es de tus antepasados su poder
que ha juntado fulgor alrededor de lodazales,
el lugar del que extrajeron el punto asertivo.
Haz valer, desde ya, tu organizada ignorancia.

6

You gave inner peace no baptistery, and for a hard-to-reckon
period you shall pay in pieces of five.

While you went from mass to the gunsmith's, stock operations
always followed one another and everything went
at the right pace, spilling oil
through the joints, rounding off the verse.
Draining waters filled the marine
basin. The garage quivered,
fees were paid. There was time for
births and crematoriums.
Why the haste? Use the time left until payment wisely.
Place a frog belly on the bruise.
Take your seat, don your glasses, say that statuesque art is
simple and sing other people's truth.
They will recognize you by the crimson of your accents.
For you have used green and pink, linden and scrub
to speak your glibness learned in silence.
You are the one who, weak and weary, carries the hercynia in his
    shield,
the bird whose feathers produce effects of light in the shadows.
Of your ancestors is its power,
which has gathered radiance around the quagmires
from where they drew the assertive point.
Assert, needless to say, your organized ignorance.

7

No te traiciones, no dejes de hacer lo que dijiste.
Allí está el camino que lleva a los oficios
aprendidos hace mucho; te agachabas y te saltaban;
se agachaban y saltabas sobre ellos.
Pasaste a gatas por entre las hendidas noches de luna.
Supuraste, sangraste por un corte ínfimo, sin dolor.
Aludiste al cóndor con el macabro juego de asociaciones.
Pero si era eso. Lanzarote el que aprendió a matar erinias.
Allá estaba la cordillera, y allá fuiste, entre viento y roca,

y cuando estabas perdido no supiste aprender nada.
Pero qué linda lejanía, aun cuando cada hora y tanto
pasaran un auto o dos, un camión petrolero.

7

Don't betray yourself; don't fail to do as you said.
This is the road that leads to trades learned
long ago. You would bend and they would jump over you;
they would bend and you would jump over them.
On all fours you crawled through the cleft moonlit nights.
You oozed, bled through a tiny cut, painless.
You alluded to the condor with the ghoulish play on associations.
But that's just what it was. Lancelot, who learned to kill Erynies.
The mountain range was there and there you went, amid wind and
     rock,

and when lost, you knew how to learn nothing.
But what nice distance, although every hour and change
a car or two would go by; a tanker truck.

8

Debería ser posible caminar por allá.
Pero encontrarías los edificios de un suburbio
y no el camino hacia los árboles y el rancho aquel,
hosco, bajo la arboleda tormentosa.
Aburridos, amarillos, grises, llovidos.
No encontrarías la tarde de verano
y los tordos, usurpadores de aquel nido.
La ciudad fue mal usada. Es usada.
En un mediodía de llovizna los edificios,
las persianas cuya pintura envejeció,
parecen resignados a su perplejidad.
Verte frente a un mar no virgen, sino desechado.
Como tordos en los nidos de otros, abandonados.

8

You ought to be able to walk around there.
But you would find suburban buildings,
not the path toward the trees and that shack,
sullen under the stormy grove.
Bored, yellow, grey, dripping.
You wouldn't find the summer afternoon
or the thrushes, usurpers of that nest.
The city was badly used. Is used.
In a drizzly midday the buildings,
the shutters of aged paint
seem resigned to their perplexity.
Standing before a sea not virgin, but refused,
like thrushes in others' nests, abandoned.

9

Fleta el barco, di las oraciones nonas, date al oleaje.
Los viste, los caminos son huellas polvorosas,
a qué negarse; navega sobre el mar que huele a fuel.
Ves que está lejano como siempre y oleoso:
conduce a la National Geographic, a los tomos
que recorriste con el esfuerzo de un grumete.
En un reumatismo que da sesgo a los gestos,
ora la túnica, ora la bota, navega y galopa
hacia los mundos artificiales sobre los que se yerguen
edificios de 300 a 400 nudos que expanden luces,
y también rejones, sobre desconocidas calas.
Hong Kong o lo que fuera; Sumatra.
Ve cómo amontonan en el negocio de pieles.
Los puertos atiborrados de contenedores rojos.
La hiperproducción de asuntos y chips,
el silencio de los aparatos, los dormidos programas.

Lavarropas en el sudeste asiático. Embalajes
entre los que se arrastran lagartijas; ligeros
latiguillos de los dioses del mar que insisten.

9

Charter the ship, say your None prayers, take to the swell.
You've seen them; the roads are dusty prints,
why say no. Sail on the sea that smells of fuel.
See, it's as distant as always, and oily;
it leads to the *National Geographic*, to the volumes
you traversed with cabin-boy effort.
Through a rheumatism that slants your gestures,
now the tunic, now the boot, sail and gallop
toward the artificial worlds supporting
three- to four-hundred–knot buildings disseminating lights,
and spikes, upon foreign coves.
Hong Kong or whatever. Sumatra.
See how they hoard in the fur business.
The ports, chock-full of red containers;
the overproduction of affairs and chips,
the silence of appliances, the sleeping software.

Washers in Southeast Asia. Packaging
amid which lizards crawl; light,
small whips of insistent sea gods.

10

Te bastaba una ciudad coloreada por el guiño
de la tormenta, el recuerdo del abrojo,
de la flor de cardo que caía en el bochorno
como un solcito blanco, despreocupado.
Eso fue hace eones. Ahora intentás pactar.
Mirás a través del vidrio opaco del pensamiento
cómo flotan hebras del paraíso de la verdad.

Bajo la lámpara difusa en la trastienda de un taller,
tendido en el catre quebrado, hacés cuentas,
utilizás números fríos, solo sentís
la noche pulida que respira en la playa de estacionamiento;
y sin embargo te preguntás cómo decir:
cómo decir con sintaxis de varias manos
lo que ha captado el cuadro, o lo que ha el cuadro
construido; si no es una, a la vez sencilla y compleja,
razón de Estado: todo lo que está allí es otra parte:
las telas de los sillones, el empapelado, el abandono
y la atención simultánea del personaje recostado.
Esplendor y crepúsculo en este cuadro del final
del diecinueve que por razones desconocidas
ocupa tu mente a las altas horas.
El lomo de un animal marítimo traza un arco fluido
en el lejano fondo de otro cuadro; hay papeles arrugados
en el piso de otro; hay sonidos en el pasillo de otro más.
La pintura ha capturado o promueve un sinfín de cosas
cuya causa de ser no es ninguna. Qué trivialidad del arte.

Como si dijera: restos que te dejan frío, o aleatorias
circunstancias. No dicen nada, nada, los pasos en la noche.

Te bastaba una ciudad coloreada por el guiño de la tormenta.
Ahora intentás pactar. Pero no hay con qué quedarse.
Entregarás un alma que no le sirve a nadie.

10

A city colored by the wink of the
storm, the memory of the burr, of the
thistle flower that fell in sultry weather
like a white, nonchalant tiny sun
were enough for you.
That was eons ago. Now you try to compromise.
Through the opaque glass of thought you look at
the floating threads of truth's paradise.

Under the dim lamp in the backroom of a studio,
lying on the broken cot you do the numbers.
You use cold figures, you only feel
the polished night that breathes in the parking lot.
And yet you wonder how to say:
How to say with the syntax of several hands
what was grasped by the painting or what the painting
built; if it isn't a simple but complex
raison d'état: everything that is there exists elsewhere —
the fabric of the armchairs, the wall paper, the simultaneous
abandonment and focus of the reclining character.
Splendor and twilight in this painting of the late
nineteenth century that for unknown reasons
occupies your mind in the small hours.
The back of a sea animal traces a fluid arc in the
distant background of another painting; there are wrinkled papers
on the floor of another; sounds in the hallway of another.
The painting has captured or promotes a myriad things
whose raison d'être is none. How trivial of art.

As if to say, remnants that do nothing for you, or random
circumstances. They say nothing, nothing, the steps in the night.

A city colored by the wink of the storm was enough.
Now you try to compromise but there's nothing to keep.
You will give up a soul that is useless.

11

El centurión silencioso en la batalla
quiere convencer a los campos que combate
por ampliar el radio de su entendimiento.
Un rayo lo ciega y piensa
que pelea en verdad por monedas.
Y que es más suyo el trigo de su tierra
que la victoria en los confines.

Puede alimentar su granja
entregando al César
el universo repetitivo: bárbaros y selvas.

11

Silently battling, the centurion
wants to convince the fields that he fights
to broaden the scope of his understanding.
Lightning blinds him, and he thinks
that he fights, in truth, for a pittance.
And the wheat from his lands is more his
than victory on the confines.

He can feed his farm
by handing Caesar
the repetitive world: barbarians and jungles.

12

Es un gran pintor Ezra, dijo el tío, sólo
que cuando el pincel está ya sin pintura
no vuelve a la paleta, lo aplica seco,
pincelada tras pincelada, seco como el río
de sus sueños, como la saturnal Castilla
que no era el planeta de sus antepasados.
De manera que no es un cuadro vacío
sino seco, sobre el que pinta todo aquello que brota
en el campo que es fantasma de su memoria, a
veces con secas pinceladas, a veces con el color
vivo de lo que ha sido vivo, ha tenido estatuto y códice.

...y el sistema de cultivo
se parecía a las leyes escritas por las que el hombre
se regía: cortaba las espadañas, cegaba al que no veía,
arrojaba a la zanja el estiércol de la palabra vana.

12

Ezra is a great painter, said his uncle, it's just that
when there's no more paint in the brush
he doesn't go back to the palette. He applies it dry,
stroke after stroke, dry like the river of his
dreams, like Saturnian Castille, which wasn't
the planet of his ancestors.
It isn't thus an empty painting but a
dry one, where he paints everything that sprouts
in the field that haunts his memory,
sometimes with dry strokes, sometimes with the
vivid color of what was alive; what had bylaws and a codex.

... and the farming system
resembled the written laws that man obeyed:
it cut the cattails, blinded those who couldn't see,
threw into the ditch the manure of vain words.

13

Cuando las persianas están bajas, usted no está.
Cuando las persianas están levantadas, está.
No, no se guíe por esto. A veces dejo las persianas
abiertas con la esperanza de que una tormenta
deje un charco en el estar. A veces cierro
las persianas porque se me de la gana.
No lo hago para burlarme de usted ni de su lógica
sencilla. Es por estos irresueltos asuntos de la mente.
Porque pienso a veces que la luz que toman las ventanas,
de noche o de día debe concentrarse, hacerse cada vez más
densa, crear un campo gravitatorio en el que yo no pueda
entrar, sino a costa de perder resistencia, contemporaneidad.

13

When the shutters are closed you are not in.
When the shutters are open you are.
No, do not guide yourself by that. Sometimes I leave
the shutters open in the hope that a storm
will leave a puddle in the parlor. Sometimes I close
the shutters because I feel like it.
I do not do it to mock you or your simple
logic but because of those unsolved issues of the mind.
Because I sometimes think the light captured by the windows
at night or during the day must concentrate, become increasingly
dense, create a gravitational field I cannot enter but at
the expense of losing resistance, contemporariness.

14

Era cacería del merodeador y ocaso de la filosofía.
Qué corno (inglés) sonaba entre los silos.
Los paisanos salían en la calesa con escopetas de caza.
Turbio, el poniente, hacía piedras oscuras y
cielos de cigüeña, mas no interesaban en el cielo
despeñaderos de lejanas épicas a los alabarderos
criollos en busca del bandido de pobre filo, ladrón
de tejas y bandolero de lavadero de lana.
Mi palabra en vano incoaba a Platón en la galería.
Era su amor el camino del guindo solitario,
larga trocha, pedregal y vuelo de tero. Aun así
hablaba diciéndole: los cipreses no son sino
longilíneos señaladores en el libro de Dios, que,
como no ignora usted, no hemos leído por las nuestras:
apenas si sus ojos, los de usted, los de tantas,
han permitido que veamos la esterilidad de sus páginas,
y, de un modo u otro, al fin y al cabo, cantáramos
precisamente los cipreses como notas exactas.
¿Entiende? ¡Lo han arruinado todo!
¡Nos han hecho platónicos!
Y ella sonreía, estrictamente en su función,
en ese escenario de ejército y gesta degradados.

14

It was the hunting of the prowler and the twilight of philosophy.
What (English) horn sounded in the silos?
The peasants rode in the buggy with hunting guns.
Murky, the sunset made dark rocks and
stork skies, yet the cliffs of remote epics in the sky
did not interest the Creole halberdiers
searching for the blunt-knife bandit, stealer
of roof tiles and fulling-mill brigand.
My words vainly brought suit against Plato on the veranda.
His love was the path of the isolated cherry tree —
long trail, scree and *tero* flight. Nonetheless,
he spoke to her saying: Cypresses are but
rangy bookmarks in God's book, which,
as you well know, we have not read by ourselves;
your eyes — yours, those of so many others —
have barely allowed us to see the aridness of its pages
and, one way or another, after all, precisely sing
cypresses as exact notes.
Do you understand? They have ruined everything!
They have rendered us Platonic!
And she smiled, strictly within her role,
in that setting of degraded armies and exploits.

15

¡Ah, orante! ¿Qué rezos? El jilguero abandonó su trono
en el árbol de trozadas ramas. Fondo de paredones
y de claraboyas industriales, donde, lo ves, también
perduran escorzos de tejados y plantas antiguas.

Todo lo que existía antes de tu nacimiento era
arcano: asimismo esas plantas, quinotos, nísperos,
el panal que escande los iluminados alejandrinos.

Recordarás a la abucla si silencio de peñas
invade esta furia que no produce nada. Malas
noches, muchos cigarrillos, tontas discusiones
sobre la trivialidad y la patria.

También la patria, Borges, carajo. El puente,
el olor de otros rellanos, de pasillos; oscura
tozudez de los días, taciturna decisión de Borbones,
de primeros ministros, de Corte y bodegón.

Días de lejía y gato acurrucado. Sinrazón de proseguir.
Pues están, fugitivos, días aplazados: mantener
la construcción del pasado, lo que debe hacerse;
el nivel de embutidos, café con coñac, el gesto.

15

Oh, supplicant! What prayers? The goldfinch left its throne
on the tree of chopped limbs. A backdrop of thick walls and
industrial skylights where, as you can see, forshortenings
of tiled roofs and old plants also persist.

Everything that existed before your birth was
arcane; likewise those plants, kumquats, loquats,
the honeycomb that scans sparkling alexandrines.

You will remember Grandmother if a silence of rocks
invades this wrath that yields nothing. Bad
nights, too many cigarettes, foolish arguments
about triviality and the fatherland.

Also the fatherland, Borges, fuck it. The bridge,
the smell of other landings, of hallways; dark
obstinacy of days, gloomy decision of Bourbon kings,
of prime ministers, of Court and taverns.

Days of bleach and curled cat. Arbitrariness of persisting.
For they are fugitives, the postponed days: Maintaining
the construction of the past, what must be done;
the number of cold meats, coffee with cognac, the gesture.

16

Si pudiera, sería lo último que haría:
pararme en el secadero de los sueños,

admirar lo que el mundo dejó junto al embarcadero,
lo que nos dio, lo verdadero.

Si pudiera sería lo último.
Despojado incluso de tu mirada.

Mirando lo que fuera que el mundo
hubiera depositado allí.

Pero lo último que haremos, ni eso
está en nuestras manos
y tal vez no esté en el corazón del mundo
la decisión de nada, ni el carozo.

16

If I could, it would be the last thing I would do:
stand in the drying room for dreams,

admire what the world left by the pier,
what it gave us, what is true.

If I could, it would be the last thing.
Deprived even of your look.

Gazing at whatever the world
had deposited there.

But the last thing we shall do, not even that
is in our hands,
and perhaps no decision, not even the pit
lies in the core of the world.

17

Cementerio de la Chacarita de los Colegiales.
Entre las tumbas hay grupos de personas.
Desentierran. De lejos son como buscadores de almejas
en el borde baboso del mar.
Uno sostiene la bolsa de plástico y el otro la llena de huesos.
Y es como el fin de las batallas.
Cuando caminan los vivos entre muertos.
Reconociendo, rematando.

17

Chacarita de los Colegiales Cemetery.
Groups of people amid the tombs.
They disinter. From afar they look like clam diggers
in the slug-like edge of the sea.
One holds the plastic bag; the other fills it with bones.
And it's like the end of a battle.
When the living walk among the dead —
identifying, finishing off.

18

Aun cuando había guerra de extermino,
Bertolt estaba seguro.
Si resultaba el cálculo, la dictadura del Partido
acabaría con el fruto agusanado de la hora.
Por eso no se paraba a mirar los abedules.
Tenía con los árboles una comunión indiferente.
Las ciudades le habían dado el sentido.
Se sentía cómodo entre pistolas y otomanas,
civilización y vanguardia,
parques y abrigos, clavos y nevisca.
En el baúl llevaba pipas y máscaras.
Sabía de qué se trataba.

18

Despite the war of extermination,
Bertolt was safe.
If calculations were right, the dictatorship of the Party
would eliminate the wormy fruit of the age.
Hence he didn't stop to look at the birches;
he had an indifferent communion with trees.
Cities had given him meaning.
He felt at ease amid guns and ottomans,
civilization and avant-garde,
parks and coats, nails and flurries.
In his trunk he carried pipes and masks.
He knew what it was about.

19

La etimología responde a la contemplatio.
Pues debe haber un rastro que una el espíritu con la cosa.
He hallado los cuadernos de observaciones del maestre.
Anotaba según el nombre que los nativos daban.

De manera que descubría en el comercio de trueque
un modo de a la vez reconocer sus acuerdos secretos
y de instilarles respeto por la zoología europea.
Y sus derivados: la botánica, las onomatopeyas,
la anáfora, las formaciones de la Copa del Mundo.

19

Etymology responds to *contemplatio*
for there must be a trace that joins the spirit with the thing.
I found the grand master's notebooks.
He wrote down the names given by the natives.

He would hence find in bartering a way to
recognize their secret agreements while
imbuing them with respect for European zoology.
And its by-products: botany, onomatopoeias,
anaphora, the line-ups for the World Cup.

20

El núcleo proletario, integrado por tejedores
y pequeños burgueses, razas inferiores
de índole industrial y comercial, pacifistas
mujeriles para, digamos, el Kaiser,
también se hizo cargo de las armas
y aprendió a manejarlas virilmente.
Así que cuando Stalin mandó dispararle un tiro
en la nuca a Zinoviev, sus oficiales y suboficiales
tenían un trato austero con las culatas.
Sus ejércitos y tiradores podían plantarse con solvencia
ante las tropas de alemanes y esgrimistas dc raza.
Como una estirpe ante otra.

20

The proletarian core, made up of weavers
and petty bourgeois, inferior races of an
industrial and commercial kind, pacifists,
womanly according to, let's say, the Kaiser,
also took charge of weapons
and learned to handle them in a manly way.
So when Stalin ordered them to shoot Zinoviev in the
nape of the neck, officers and petty officers
showed an austere manner with the butts of their guns.
His armies and shooters could capably stand firm
before the troops of Germans and born fencers.
Like one bloodline facing another.

21

Es indiferente que con alegría campesina
los rojos dispararan el "órgano de Stalin".
La cuestión de que un obrero de base
haya diseñado el mejor fusil de las futuras guerras
es también un hecho menor.
Cuando se paraban frente a la mesa de arena
o cuando manejaban el plomo y el abastecimiento
en el terreno de las operaciones,
los generales del Partido eran eficientes y célebres.

21

That the reds would shoot "Stalin's organ" with
peasant joy is immaterial.
That a rank-and-file worker
would design the best gun of future wars
is a minor detail, too.
When standing at the sand table
or when handling the lead and supplies
in the field of operations,
the Party generals were efficient and acclaimed.

22

Si he de morir, que calce los zapatos de tu abuelo.
No vi mejor diseño en mucho tiempo. Finos y lúgubres.
Los tenés bajo la mesa de vidrio del living
con otros remanentes, como cajas, pinceles chinos.
También tenés un cuchillo de artillero.
Pero esto no ha terminado.
Porque me gustaría enjugar con la manga
el vapor pegado al vidrio, mirar la calle antes de salir,
con el gesto de un personaje de Dickens
que se mueve en una ciudad poderosa.
"Yo mismo estoy de capa caída en este momento,
pero puedo invitarlo con un plato de comida".

22

Should I die, I must wear your grandfather's shoes.
Haven't seen a better style in a long time — fine and doleful.
You'll find them under the glass table in the living room
with other remainders such as boxes, Chinese paint brushes.
You also have a machine gunner's knife.
But that is not all.
For I'd like to wipe with my sleeve
the steam stuck to the glass, look at the street before I leave
with the gesture of a Dickensian character
moving around in a powerful city.
"I too am in low spirits at the moment,
but I can offer you a plate of food."

23

Los esclavos huían por las estepas acribilladas
con el quizás y la vida, aunque en despojos.
Sintieron el pánico ante los Panzer
y el olor de la sangre.
En un segundo ponían en la balanza
la duda en el triunfo final
y el estar en el hospital canalizados y oyendo
los quejidos de los camaradas
y la voz del comisario político, una certeza.
O muertos, carroña indiferente a la victoria.
Así, retrocedieron pero no cntrcgaron sus ciudades.
La aldea sí, la égloga, Esenin, el fuego y la piara.
Su origen y sus madres. No el Kremlin.
No las pútridas cañerías de Stalingrado.
Resistieron como ratas, con el culo expuesto a sus generales
y el disparo de los propios que seguía a los desertores.
Avanzaron con el invierno entre cadáveres y trazadoras.
Y entre dientes decían que la huída es vaguedad.
El que escapa de verdad deja su cuerpo
a los cuervos y al juicio del Partido.

23

Slaves fled through the bullet-riddled steppes
with a perhaps and their lives, though in tatters.
They panicked before the Panzers and the
smell of blood.
In a second they weighed their
doubts about a final victory
and being in the hospital with an IV
while hearing their comrades moaning
and the voice of the commissar, a certainty.
Or dead, carrion oblivious to victory.
So they retreated without surrendering their cities.
The village, yes, the eclogue, Essenin, the fire and the herd;
their origin and their mothers. Not the Kremlin.
Not the putrid pipes of Stalingrad.
They resisted like rats, their ass exposed to their generals
and to the shots of their own side chasing deserters.
They moved forward with the winter amid corpses and tracers.
And muttered that fleeing is vague.
He who truly escapes leaves his body
to the crows and a Party trial.

24

Durante las noches no fuiste acechado.
Estabas entre la suma restricción de los forzados.
Cada uno de los que dormían en sus departamentos
veía sombras o fuego en sueños o despertaba
mirando sus manos, su cuerpo, como vos,
iluminados por la lamparita tenue, el sudor amarillo.

24

At night you were not stalked.
You were amid the supreme constraints of the convicted.
Each of those who slept in their apartments
saw shadows or fire in his dreams or awoke
looking at his hands, his body, like you,
lit by the dim lightbulb, the yellow sweat.

25

Lo que condenan a tu alrededor es la muerte joven.
Con malicia has preguntado si a la muerte o al que muere.
¿Es honorable llegar a viejo y hartarse de comida?
¿No es honorable fumar y enfermarse de gripe española?
A mis setenta años seguiré haciendo muecas.
Pues las palabras son equívocas
cuando el anochecer se levanta.

25

What is being condemned around you is young death.
Maliciously, you ask whether death or the dying.
Is it honorable to reach old age and gorge oneself with food?
Isn't it honorable to smoke and contract the Spanish flu?
At seventy I will continue to make face gestures.
For words are ambiguous
when the twilight rises.

26

Sí, es pertinente sentarse con el saco puesto.
Primero en el living amplio en el que se habla,
aún con cierto embarazo, de la noticia del día
(en el campo literario, pues de esto se trata,
es noticia el desplante de una viuda).
Después en el antiguo comedor se discute a fondo
el estado real del imperio; si declina, si todavía la fuerza lo asiste.

Con el café, nuevamente en el living,
se comentan poemarios y citas recién adquiridas.
Seguimos con el saco puesto, las piernas cruzadas.
La calidad del vino se menciona de paso
y el anfitrión, como se debe, agradece ligeramente.
Tres de los comensales sabían manejar los cubiertos.
El cuarto, lo hacía con aceptable habilidad,
excepto cuando lo turbaba la idea de que era
el único con relaciones en la CIA y, tal vez,
el único que conocía a fondo la batalla de Stalingrado.
El quinto, adinerado, hundía el cuchillo en la presa
con el ahínco de las chabolas y los campamentos.
Si tienes fuerzas por detrás de los sitiadores,
resiste, pues la victoria será tuya. No puedes,
dijo Saladino, iniciar un sitio con fuerzas a tus espaldas.
El cerrojo se cerró sobre Von Paulus.
Es producto de esta civilización el cultivo de la vid,
  aquel tapado de armiño y la forma de recordarte.

26

Yes, it is relevant to sit with one's jacket on.
First in the ample living room where one talks,
with some awkwardness still, about the news of the day
(in the literary field, for this is the topic,
the rudeness of a widow is newsworthy).
Then in the old-fashioned dining room the actual state of
the empire is thoroughly discussed. If it's in decline,
if strength still assists it.

Over coffee, back in the living room,
poetry books and recently acquired quotes are shared.
We keep our jackets on, our legs crossed.
The quality of the wine is briefly mentioned,
and the host, as is fitting, offers a light thank-you.
Three of the diners knew how to use their silverware.
The fourth did it with reasonable skill,
save when he was disturbed by the notion that he was
the only one with connections to the CIA, and perhaps
the only one deeply familiar with the battle of Stalingrad.
The fifth, well-off, buried his knife in his prey
with the eagerness of slums and tents.
If you have troops behind the besiegers
resist, as victory is yours. You cannot,
said Saladin, start a siege with forces at your rear.
The circle closed on Von Paulus.
They are all products of our civilization — vineyard growing,
that ermine coat, and the way to remember you.

27

El chirrido de una jauría debió decirles de la noche
más dobleces que los círculos concéntricos de los sistemas visibles.
Pues no era signo el cielo estrellado, sino la pura plenitud.
En cambio, el lejano ladrido penetrante fue la mezcla
de un metal impalpable deducido en el infierno.
Con las mismas nociones se pertrecharon los nómades,
y el asedio de chacal de sus cimeras
reducía las variables a esta monotemática cuestión:
la inteligencia no dará cuenta de los significados
sino de las plantas viciosas trepadas a los últimos farallones.

Dicho de otro modo, el planeta es sencillo,
plano; la piel extendida de un cadáver o el vellocino
en cuyo envés se escribió el mapa de la Quimera.

Lo ven bien cuando observan desde las altas islas de un feriado.
Con el faltante vinieron los malos sueños
y el quizá seguro detrás de cualquier puerta.
Había signos en las miradas de los depósitos
y en el modo en que caían en el mar los restos desde los trinquetes.
Basura de intelecto.
Incluso, las frías invasiones, el invierno en las correderas.

27

About the night, the squeal of a pack must have told them
more folds than concentric circles of the visible systems.
For the starry sky was not sign but sheer plenitude.
The faraway, penetrating bark, by contrast, was the mixture
of an impalpable metal deducted in hell.
The nomads supplied themselves with the same notions,
and the jackal-like siege of their crests
reduced the variables to this monothematic issue:
Intelligence will not account for meaning
but for vicious plants climbing the last cliffs.

In other words, the planet is simple, flat —
the stretched skin of a corpse or the fleece
on whose back the map of the Chimera was written.

They see it distinctly when watching from the tall islands of a holiday.
With lack came the bad dreams
and the safe "perhaps" behind all doors.
There were signs in the looks of the deposits and in the way
remains fell to the sea from the foremasts.
Debris of the intellect.
Including cold invasions, winter in the chip logs.

28

Puso el pie entre el caniche y una mujer
para bajar el escalón hacia la calle
cuando pasó ante sus ojos ese rostro joven desfigurado
por un lampazo de rápidas galaxias.

Suele hablarse de las pinturas fáciles con gramática compleja.
A este Bacon que se interpuso entre el perro trivial
y la imagen de la vacua vereda de enfrente
nada es posible agregar.

En los ojos no había desesperación
y la mandíbula se iba hacia el Oriente
mientras pasaba oteando el mundo de los otros
aquella figura concebida con apuro por el dolor indiferente

—vencido por las sociales cuestiones de una Cartago
en llamas, abrumado por la clásica escultura
de un Prometeo entregado a los buitres, conmovido
por la furia de los pobres, el pintor estaba ausente.
Solo Bacon pudo haber dicho: ella está en el orden
de los planetas que os abandonan.

28

He placed his foot between the poodle and a woman
to climb down the step toward the street
when that young face disfigured by
a mopping of fast galaxies passed before his eyes.

We tend to discuss easy paintings with complex grammar.
To this Bacon that came between the trivial dog
and the image of the vacuous opposite sidewalk
nothing can be added.

The eyes showed no despair,
and the jaw went toward the East
while that figure conceived in haste by
indifferent pain passed by, scanning the world of others

— defeated by the social matters of a burning
Carthage, overwhelmed by the classical sculpture
of a Prometheus surrendered to the vultures, moved
by the fury of the poor, the painter was absent.
Only Bacon could have said: She dwells in the order
of the planets that abandon you.

29

Un sonido convierte a la ciudad en maderamen.
Así es como resiste el bien los ataques del desierto.
En las dunas se inclina ante un hoyo provisorio
quien sabe que el viento es su padre madre
y su legítimo hermano.

Cuando huye la ciudad como una nave
en su lugar resisten los acantilados
de los antiguos muertos provisorios.

Pero una vez más mira al nómada rodeado
del halcón y el hipogrifo, de parcas y racimos.

Este es el que ahora hablará y preguntará los motivos
por los que incesantemente construyen y demuelen
troyas, babilonias, tebas, establos y mercados
—tu propio fantasma se sentará a tu mesa otra vez; insistirá:
no escribas.

29

A sound turns the city into timber.
That's how good resists the onslaughts of the desert.
In the dunes, in front of a temporary hole
bend those who know that the wind is their father mother
legitimate brother.

When the city flees like a vessel,
in its place resist the cliffs of the
ancient provisional dead.

Yet once again they watch the nomad surrounded by
hawk and hippogriff, parcae and grapes.

This is the one who will now speak and ask the reasons why
troys, babylons, thebes, stables and markets
are incessantly built and demolished.
Your own ghost will sit once again at your table; it will insist:
Don't write.

30

Soy el escriba del Partido y de los documentos desclasificados.
Escuchad los que no han podido hablar.
Con sangre de mongoles, de ucranios y de eslavos suicidas
se alzaron las columnas de humo del triunfo vuestro.
De los campos de la horda salió el acero que permite
la victoria de los burgers, el relativismo y el ocio.
Antes del día D estuvieron los días Z del Frente Oriental.
Allá se amasó en sangre y pantanos nevados este día hueco.
Con un viva Stalin en la boca se iban los muertos.
Habéis visto películas de la sangre y el miedo
pero poco supisteis del Frente Oriental.
Antes que la carnicería del Canal estuvieron
los millones de muertos del Frente Oriental.

Honor, camaradas de estiércol,
a los muertos del Frente Oriental.
Cada bocado y risa y zumbido de autopista
se lo debéis a los camaradas del Frente Oriental.

30

I am the scribe of the Party and of declassified files.
Listen, those who have not been able to speak.
The blood of suicide Mongols, Ukranians, and Slavs
built the smoke columns of your triumph.
From the fields of the horde came the steel that allows
the victory of burgers, relativism and leisure.
Before D-day were the Z days of the Eastern Front.
There, this hollow day was kneaded with blood and snowy
        marshes.
The dead would go with a "long live Stalin" in their mouths.
You watched films of blood and fear
but knew little about the Eastern Front.
Before the slaughter of the Channel
millions were dead on the Eastern Front.

Honor, comrades of manure,
to the dead of the Eastern Front.
Each bite and laugh and highway whirr
you owe to the comrades of the Eastern Front.

31

Hablo de los tiempos del conquistador y de los veranos perdidos.
Pueden creer que esto es poco para oda, porque necesito el okay
de un lenguaje fluido.

Comieron cuero y ratas para fundar almacenes y curtiembres.
Engendraron para traer revoluciones de pacotilla.
Y sin embargo, ejércitos.

31

I'm talking about the time of the conqueror and lost summers.
You may think this isn't much for an ode, since I need the green light
of fluid language.

They ate leather and rats to create general stores and tanneries.
They procreated to produce two-bit revolutions.
And yet, armies.

32

Ningún Eldorado. Sólo las olas y la baba de los muertos.
Ningún latido de plata ni de oro. Sólo monedas opacas.
Ah, sí, imposible de creer. Meses de navegación oleosa,
no por un sueño, pues aquellos cráneos no soñaban.
Buscaban la lavada claridad de las cosas.
Rezaban al cañón y morían en los pastos.

¿Lo veis? El pájaro volando en círculos sobre la loma.
Imposible llamar a eso collado. Aquí, sin cesar,
y en cada minuto, cambian las palabras.
Al norte, llamarán aquestas "cuchillas"
y, al pájaro, "garza mora" o "gallareta."

32

No Eldorado; only waves, and the dribble of the dead.
No silver or gold beat; only opaque coins.
Oh, yes, impossible to believe. Months of oily sailing;
not for a dream, for those skulls did not dream.
They sought the washed-out clarity of things.
They prayed to the cannon and died in the grass.

Can you see it? The bird circling the hillock.
Impossible to call that a hill. Here words change
endlessly and by the minute.
In the North they will call them *cuchillas*,
and the bird, *garza mora* or *gallareta*.

33

Alzaga, que sería almacenero, el boticario Arriola,
el herrero de Cádiz, el lector de sentencias,
el alabardero que fue mozo de cuadra,
el gitano devenido artillero,
el cazador de liebres hecho capitán,
el fontanero cubierto de armaduras,
el que portaba cinco o más muertes a navaja.
el sacristán, el que arropaba perros.

¿Arte aquí? ¿A quién le cuadra?
Ni gloria ni imperio.
A crear chabolas y aldeas en damero.
Humo de velas y olor de grasa.
Y sin embargo, ejércitos.

33

Alzaga, who would become a grocer, Arriola the chemist,
the blacksmith from Cádiz, the reader of judgments,
the halberdier who had been a stable boy,
the gypsy turned gunner,
the erstwhile hare hunter, now captain,
the plumber covered in armor,
the one who boasted five or more knife deaths,
the sacristan, the one who tucked in dogs.

Art, here? It suits whom?
Neither glory nor empire.
Go create slums and grid-patterned towns.
The smoke of candles and the smell of grease.
And yet, armies.

34

Bien, fue vuestra hora, lo digo en nombre de los míos.
Ellos vinieron después con olor a cuerpo.
Lo digo por mi abuela contemplando la nevada de 1918,
por Lucania y los trojes de Castilla la vieja.
Habéis esparcido la gangrena y el trigo, de carambola
llenasteis de vacas un desierto.
Padres de cabeza de ajo:
toda esta navegación por un huerto.
Un continente en el que cagar y sembrar.
Lo hicisteis por las razones de Castilla y Aragón,
que se reducen a manteca y atavíos.
Pero fue vuestra la hora.

Y sin embargo, ejércitos.

34

Well, it was your hour, I say it on behalf of my people.
They came later smelling of bodies.
I speak for my grandmother, watching the snowfall of 1918,
for Lucania and the barns of Old Castile.
You spread gangrene and wheat, serendipitously
filled a desert with cows.
Garlic-head parents:
all that sailing for a garden.
A continent where to shit and plant.
You did it for the reasons of Castille and Aragon,
which boil down to butter and clothing.
But the hour was yours.

And yet, armies.

Esta tierra no es la tierra de mis muertos.
Ellos lo fueron bajo las botas de sicarios.
Cayeron bajo la alambrada cuando los tártaros.
Vendedores de autos usados y comedores de crustáceos
son ahora la estirpe que me ofrecéis elegir.
Decid: ¿cómo unos conspiradores de botica
me han dado ardor y recuerdo de arado?
— y sin embargo, ejércitos —
El coselete, el peto, el espaldar,
rápido ennegrecen, y un campo de duros y sofaifas
presiona sobre los conjurados.
Pedradas, módico clamoreo, cuestión de cabildo y corte.
Y más tarde,
ejércitos.

Ahí tenéis por fin el dorado y el azul. La cabeza cetrina
se ha iluminado frente a las armas de un auténtico genio.
Ahora, si me lo permitís, el himno.
Románticos han desenterrado Grecia.
Por fin, ejércitos.
A lomo de mula bajo la grandeza del cóndor funebrero.

35

This land is not the land of my dead.
They went under the boots of hired killers.
They fell under the wire fence when the Tartars.
Used car salesmen and shellfish eaters,
they are now the lineage you offer me to choose.
Tell me, how could some chemist's shop conspirators
give me passion and memories of the plough?
And yet, armies.
Corselet, breastplate, back
quickly darken, and a field of toughs and losers
closes in on the confederates.
Rocks thrown, modest clamor, a matter of town hall and court.
And later
armies.

Behold finally the gold and the blue. The sallow head
enlightened before the weapons of a true genius.
Now, if you allow me, the anthem.
The Romantics have unearthed Greece.
And finally, armies.
On mules, under the greatness of the undertaker condor.

La luz grisácea los acompañó y no ignoraron
que vendría, con las armas y el pendón,
el descubrimiento.

Un sabio se inclinó sobre el paisaje.
Esto, musitó, no se llama América.
Esto se llama el río, el perro empiojado.
Esto se llama arreo y luces gordas.
Esto se llama la pampa, el galopito,
el corral, el vino áspero, la tuna.

Esto se llama entubamiento.
El agua del arroyito cae en la cloaca pulposa.
Aquí nací. Allá estaba la fábrica amarilla.
Aquí el árbol aquel, y allá la laguna.
Tuve una anguila en una bolsa.
Tuve un rancho. Balas de avión de 1955.
Las lluvias del sudeste a veces inclinadas.
Entonces las claraboyas se pusieron negras.
En el suburbio un Chevrolet pausado
respiraba de tarde en tarde, acatarrado.
Y un tipo salía de la sombra
con sonrisa de muerto.

36

The greyish light was with them, and they could not but
know that with standard and weapons would come
discovery.

A wise man leaned over the landscape.
This, he murmured, is not called America.
This is called river, lice-infested dog.
This is called herding and thick lights.
This is called the Pampas, short gallop,
pen, harsh wine, cactus fig.

This is called piping.
The water of the brook falls into the fleshy sewers.
I was born here. The yellow factory was there.
Here that tree, there the pond.
I had an eel in a bag.
I had a cabin. 1955 plane bullets.
The southeast rains, slanted at times.
Then the skylights turned black.
In the suburbs a slow-paced Chevy
breathed from time to time, congested.
And a guy came out of the shadows
with a dead man's smile.

37

Permitidme: no olvidé nada.
Pero nada recuerdo.
El crepúsculo recuerdo.
Las casas con letrinas.
Hilos delgados de araña o de sótano o pintura
o de luz de clavos o de la palabra nieto
o de rosales grises o de árboles cariados.
O de gotas pesadas o de sol en un alfeizar
o de gallinas o de un halcón de campo;

hilos de cosas y sustancias
y de últimas horas en invierno
tejieron algo más que recuerdo:
tendones en el movimiento casual,
pulmones en los que suenan las palabras.

37

Allow me; I forgot nothing.
Yet there's nothing I remember.
The twilight I remember.
Houses with latrines.
Thin threads of spiders or cellars or paint
or shining nails or the word grandchild
or grey rose bushes or decayed trees.
Or heavy drops or sun on a windowsill
or hens or a country falcon;

threads of things and matter
and last winter hours
have woven more than memories;
tendons in casual movement,
lungs where words resound.

38

Soy el que aprendió gramática
para leer las etiquetas de los frascos.
Yodo, árnica, azogue, benceno.
Un hombre de cincuenta y tantos al sol.
La muerte era nuestra profesión;
la decisión, el libro dócil.

Supieron aquella tradición:
almuerzos en el Almirantazgo,
mensajes de Bombay,
el trazado de la batalla sobre el mantel.
La sobremesa sin migas ni máculas.

Miré en los arrugados rostros de los generales rojos
y la revelación sobrevino y regresó a sus fueros.
Tronó la frontera como una tormenta.
Lejos. Lejos de sus decisiones.
Lejos de los labios tensos y de las medallas.
Y de la helada sintaxis de la pólvora.

Penetró su insistencia la arquitectura de Dios.
Pero no salieron indemnes de allí.
La situación los hizo para sí mismos incomprensibles.
Ganaron la guerra y perdieron las ciudades.
Se cubrió de pústulas el contorno de la conquista.

Autos detenidos frente al Estado Mayor.
Las gaviotas suspendidas sobre el río congelado.
El ordenanza comiendo a hurtadillas el sándwich de paté.

I'm the one who learned grammar
to read the labels on jars.
Iodine, arnica, quicksilver, benzene.
A fifty-plus-old man in the sun.
Death was our trade.
Decision, the docile book.

They knew that tradition:
lunches at the Admiralty,
messages from Bombay,
charting the battle on the tablecloth.
The after-dinner chat, immaculate and crumbless.

I looked into the wrinkled faces of the Red generals,
and the revelation swiftly appeared and returned to its roots.
The border rumbled like a storm.
Far away; far from their decisions;
far from the tense lips and the medals.
And the icy syntax of gunpowder.

Their insistence pierced God's architecture.
Yet they did not leave unscathed.
The situation turned them ungraspable to themselves.
They won the war and lost the towns.
Pustules covered the outline of the conquest.

Halted cars in front of the General Staff.
Suspended seagulls over the frozen river.
The orderly stealthily eating a paté sandwich.

39

Ha perdido la flor de la mirada y su hacienda.
Cholo de ojos ingenuos y chaleco de alpaca
apoyado en su bastón, comprende su desamparo.
La deriva de las cosas lo trajo al barrio.
Mueve entre sus dedos llaves ennegrecidas:
"He sido príncipe del carrascal.
Removí tierra y guano, mis cuentas
bancarias alimentan polillas. Llegué
en un Packard azul a las puertas de Lima.

Sonaron cuernos y bailé en la enramada.
Miré mis zapatos amarillos: no obran milagro.
Perplejo en el garaje espero en vano."

De su simpleza sale rodeado de luz untosa, digno.
Pero en momento alguno tuvo un sueño,
un final, un objetivo, un soplo, una trascendencia.

39

He lost the flower in his eyes, and his ranch.
A Cholo of naive eyes in alpaca vest,
leaning on his stick, understands his helplessness.
Drifting things brought him to the neighborhood.
He shifts blackened keys between his fingers:
"I've been prince of the oak grove,
dug up soil and guano, my bank accounts are
feeding the moths. I arrived in a blue
Packard at the gates of Lima.

Horns blew, and I danced in the arbor.
I looked at my yellow shoes — they perform no miracle.
Puzzled, I wait in vain in the garage."

He comes out of his simplicity surrounded by greasy light,
    dignified.
Yet at no moment did he have a dream,
an ending, a goal, a breath, a transcendence.

40

Enfundados en criterios infalibles,
los tanquistas, los fusileros, los sin grietas,
en realidad peleaban por la imaginación,
devenir del piélago de ambiciones machacadas
en el entrenamiento, jugo, sustancia
que hacía una cuestión concreta
de todo aquello que se llamaba Algo:
si existe el concepto de Patria, hay Patria;
si existe el concepto de Dios, hay Dios.

40

Wrapped in infallible criteria,
tank crews, fusiliers, the solid ones
actually fought for imagination,
the progress of the deep sea of ambitions crushed
during training, juice, substance
turning everything called Something
into a concrete situation:
if the notion of Fatherland exists, there is a Fatherland;
if the notion of God exists, there is a God.

41

Los mataron y mataron.
Deben saber que el que pierde la vida,
pierde cualquier cosa vacía,
desde todo punto de vista amada,
mantenida con fuego de ramas
y con negruras rebañadas
de utensilios de caza.

Pierde el estar, la terminal nerviosa
en la que se enciende lo que quiere
encenderse: el filo de una visera,
ribetes de un sillón, una estridente risa,
el trabajo de unas raíces en el fondo de la vereda.

41

They were killed and they killed.
They must know that he who loses his life
loses any empty thing,
beloved from every point of view,
maintained by a bonfire
and scraped blacknesses of hunting gear.

He loses the being there, the nerve ending
where what wants to glow
will glow: the edge of a visor,
trims of an armchair, a strident laugh,
the work of some roots deep under the sidewalk.

42

Sí, el pensamiento es el centro del infierno.
Rey en una ciudad de color de bronce,
con costras de basura en las calles.
Multitud y tránsito de chatarra, urinarios podridos,
cementerios removidos, aullidos de despeñados.

"Soy el iluminado por la luz de las llagas
y mi energía proviene de la ciudad asfixiada
y de los estertores entre sábanas que nadie cambia".
"Me han ungido el Partido, el Derecho Civil
y la voluntad de Baal, que destroza a los caídos".
"La organización en torno al versículo primero".

42

Yes, thought is the core of hell.
King in a city the color of bronze
with scabs of waste on the streets.
Crowds and junk traffic, rotten urinals,
dug-up cemeteries, the howling of those plunging into the ravine.

"I've been kindled by the light of the sores,
and my energy stems from the suffocated city
and from death rattles between unchanged sheets."
"I was anointed by the Party, Civil Law
and the will of Baal, which crushes the fallen."
"Organizing around the first verse."

43

¿Cómo mantener el dominio del mar?
Lleno al fin de negros y mercaderes,
por siglos barrenado, navegado, instilado de sangre.
Sin embargo, aún carcome las ideas de poder
junto con los desperdicios y los naufragios.

Mi reino ha caído en una isla de excrementos.
He plantado mi torreón y cubrí la espada
con matas secas, con plumas y vísceras.
Con eficacia, construí un observatorio.
Vigilo los movimientos cíclicos en un radio de 20 estadios.

43

How to maintain control of the sea?
Full at last with negroes and traders,
drilled, sailed, instilled with blood for centuries.
And yet it still corrodes notions of power
along with waste and shipwrecks.

My kingdom has fallen on an island of feces.
I planted my turret and covered my sword
with dry shrubs, feathers and viscera.
Adeptly, I built an observatory.
I watch cyclical movements in a 20-furlong radius.

44

Órdenes del Servicio Secreto de la Corona:
ceder dos palmos, un topo, cuatro maravedíes.
Retroceder en orden hasta el Libro Cuarto.
Armar el pináculo de la gloria.
Aguardar el chaparrón. Cubrirse de lapas.
En el fango hasta la cintura probar la resistencia imperial.
Dar al romanticismo la cerca de cañas
y los caminos que llevan a los nidos y las habichuelas.
No será dicho el día. No habrá señales.
No abandonen el terreno, la zona del dolor.

44

Orders of the Crown's secret service:
surrender two hands, a mole, four maravedis.
Retreat in order as far as Book Four.
Build the pinnacle of glory.
Await the downpour. Cover yourselves with limpets.
With mud up to your waist, prove imperial resistance.
Leave to romanticism the cane fence and the
roads leading to nests and beans.
The day will not be named. There will be no signs.
Do not leave the grounds, the zone of pain.

45

Resumen Quinto: volvimos al río por cangrejos.
Sopas de noche y friegas por la mañana.
Dominio absoluto de la autopista.
Dos baterías sobre el puente y provisiones de boca.
Venta de mobiliario y equipo gastronómico.
Deserciones intelectuales sin consecuencias.

"He tenido un día satisfactorio. Controlo cierta región.
Duermo con una certeza. Me despierto a las nueve.
Tengo café y manteca.
Pero debo dar un paso más, Watson.
Es innecesario, totalmente presuntuoso.
Encuentro un desajuste entre la vida y lo vivo.
Debería ser capaz de fumar y andar en bata
en esta cima de la propiedad, de la construcción.
No hay, fíjese, ruidos en el desván
y en Londres los diagramas están activos.
La guerra ha sido siempre auxiliar para nosotros.
La frenología nos ofrece un prospecto suficiente".

45

Fifth Brief: we went back to the river for crabs.
Soup in the evening and rubs in the morning.
Absolute control of the highway.
Two batteries on the bridge, and victuals.
Furniture and restaurant equipment for sale.
Inconsequent intellectual desertions.

"I had a satisfactory day. I control a certain region.
I sleep with one certainty, wake up at nine,
have my coffee and butter ready.
But I must take another step, Watson.
It is unnecessary, utterly presumptuous.
I find a discrepancy between life and the living.
I ought to be able to smoke and wear a robe in this
peak of property, of construction.
There's no noise in the attic, mind you,
and charts are active in London.
The war has always been ancillary to us.
Phrenology offers us enough information."

46

"Evitad a la prensa. En el gas de las tormentas
escribid.
"Marciales, honrosos, venid a por la paga
con vuestro cráneo en la mano.
"No sois nada, nadie.
"Debéis no serlo.
"Esta es la voz del estadio inundado.
"Aquí alzáis el trofeo, fantasmas,
y la porcelana de vuestros dientes,
la ajustada sincronización de vuestros organismos,
esa repetida maravilla,
fue un don que debía extinguirse.
"Lo usasteis en el amartillar de los máuser
y en el ágil desplazamiento por zanjas
y campos roturados por los morteros.
"Esta es, aunque no parezca, la gloria del soldado.
"No la ebanistería de los ministerios
ni las salvas entre lápidas y vuelo de tordos."

Esas luces allá, detrás del humo aquel,
¿son la ciudad?
¿Éste es el Velódromo, aquél
el tanque de gas;
éste, el distribuidor de la autopista?

46

"Avoid the press. In the storm gas,
write.
"Martial, honorable, claim your pay
skull in hand.
"You are nothing, nobody.
"You must not be that.
"This is the voice of the flooded stadium.
"Here you raise the trophy, ghosts,
and the porcelain of your teeth,
the accurate syncronization of your bodies,
that repeated wonder,
was a gift that must die out.
"You used it in the cocking of rifles
and the agile journey through ditches
and fields plowed by mortars.
"It may not seem so, but this is the soldiers' glory.
"Not the woodwork of the ministries,
nor the salvos among tombstones and thrush flights."

Those lights over there, behind that smoke,
are they the city?
Is this the cycle track,
that, the gas tank,
this, the highway junction?

47

Resumen Sexto: catedrático en la mesa de cocina,
frente al pingüe regalo de una ventana y el fresco.
Más tarde, en la calle, detenido por el semáforo
mira el árbol de corteza oscura que se abisma en su color.
En tal profundidad suenan lanzas,
la pampa se mueve hacia Carhué.
Y no es todo, hay tropas con mantos cenicientos
bajo nevisca en los pantanos de un reino bárbaro.
Y no es todo.

Este reino fue comadreja y voladera.
La balanza del buhonero y el remington.
Ese árbol, devorado en un segundo por el olvido,
no fue plantado aquí, creció entre grietas y abadías,
solitario, en peñascos y apartado del bosque junto a un camino.
Pero en este y en otros tiempos.
Y hoy alguien se detuvo ante él.
Expuso haber leído que tal vez estamos presos en un nudo de
     tiempo.
¿Y cómo lo sabrá si ha perdido ese árbol?

47

Sixth Brief: professor at the kitchen table
before the rich gift of a window and fresh air.
Later, on the street, stopped by the red light,
he watches the tree of somber bark plunge into its darkness.
In such depth lances clang,
the Pampas shift toward Carhué.
And that is not all; there are troops with ash-grey cloaks
under a flurry in the swamps of a barbaric kingdom.
And that is not all.

This kingdom was weasel and paddle.
The peddler's scale and the Remington 1866.
That tree, devoured in a flash by oblivion
was not planted here; it grew between cracks and abbeys,
solitary, in boulders and far from the woods next to a road.
But in this and other times.
And today someone stopped before it.
He expounded on having read that we might be trapped in a time
    knot.
And how will he know that if he has lost the tree?

48

Las trabajosas migraciones, no el malón.
El horizonte, de pastos infestado.
Los que llegaron solos, ilegales.
Sus huesos blanqueando en los pantanos
o los ojos con que miran desde los rellanos
de edificios públicos.

Así, el imperio fue minado.
No por la incursión de la horda:
por su propio fulgor
que atrajo desterrados,
sombras desde los osarios
creados por las centurias en terrenos bárbaros.

Bajo las arcadas, entre las achuras del circo
el nubarrón de sueño y pesadilla
se alzó hasta las estatuas y el Senado.
Roma, Washington, la central Europa
cayeron, caen, mueren entre heces y pocilgas.

Aun así, las cosas. Paredes de rojo calamar.
La esquina y las persianas que se levantan
y caen con regularidad mecánica.
Los días del calendario, la tarde del sábado.
La música que se oye en el traspatio.
Tipos con herramientas en los techos.
Mantenimiento, partes meteorológicos, zapatos.
La hora del gato; la hora del mono;
medianoche: la hora de la rata.

48

Painstaking migrations, not the Indian raid.
The horizon, by grass infested.
Those who arrived alone, illegal;
their bones blanching in the swamps
or the eyes with which they stare from the landings
of public buildings.

Thus was the empire weakened.
Not by the invasion of the horde;
by its own brilliance,
which drew in the banished,
shadows from the ossuaries
created by the Roman army in barbarian land.

Under the arcade, amid the entrails of the circus,
the storm cloud of dreams and nightmares
rose up to the statues and the Senate.
Rome, Washington, Central Europe
fell, fall, die amid feces and pigsties.

Even so, things. Squid-red walls.
The corner and the shutters that open
and close with machinelike regularity.
The days in the calendar, Saturday afternoon.
Music heard in the backyard.
Guys with tools on the roofs.
Maintenance, weather forecasts, shoes.
The hour of the cat; the hour of the monkey;
midnight; the hour of the rat.

49

Ah la torre de los albigenses en el barranco del despeñadero.
De ella parten aún tiros de gracia que no hallarán destino.
Rodeada de desiertos pintados o corredores humosos, el gris
domina su semblante en el que a veces destella una esmeralda.

Saluda al entregar el diario fragante, las hojas
que se marchitarán en el baño.
La ofrenda del vendedor de periódicos
como la verdad y su rápida disolución.

49

Oh the tower of the Albigenses on the drop of the cliff.
From there still fly finishing shots that will find no destination.
Surrounded by painted deserts or smoky hallways,
    grey dominates its
countenance where at times an emerald will sparkle.

He says hello while delivering the fragrant paper, pages
that will wither in the bathroom.
The offer of the newspaper salesman,
like truth and its quick dissolution.

50

Poderoso es el designio. Cada vez que se atisbe la verdad
se multiplicarán los floreros, las candelas, las fiestas,
la relatividad del confort o de las penurias sufridas
por la familia, la estirpe, la raza, el partido.
Atila, en su Porsche, recorre la ciudad que insiste en aniquilarse.
Ha salido indemne de los quejidos del vencido y del
    remordimiento.
El estado de eterna destrucción es su certeza. No hay fin.
Nunca morirán del todo los otros, ni él, ni sus cortejos.
Ha leído los signos en el mismo fondo de tormenta,
siglo tras siglo y masacre tras masacre.
Se ha retirado, impotente y colérico, pues
nada en la historia dependió de su poder sangriento.
La máquina hubiese funcionado de todos modos.
El auto se pierde en la niebla ojerosa de la autopista.
Su gesta son escenas de una película mal copiada.
Su rostro decae en el bien escaso, se inflama en la sombra.
Y no es suyo, es el del asesino en el diario, el del tunante,
el del florista o el del héroe circunstancial del balompié.

50

Design is powerful. Every time the truth is glimpsed
vases, tapers, feasts will multiply,
as will the relativity of comfort or misfortunes suffered
by the family, the lineage, the race, the Party.
In his Porsche, Attila crosses the city that insists on wiping itself
    out.
He has come out unscathed from the moaning of the vanquished
    and remorse.
The state of eternal destruction is his certainty. There is no end.
Never will the others fully die, nor him, nor his retinues.
He has read the signs in the same storm backdrop,
century after century, massacre after massacre.
He has left, impotent and furious,
for nothing in history depended on his bloody power.
The machine would have worked regardless.
The car vanishes in the haggard fog of the highway.
His quest is scenes of a poorly copied film.
His face withers in the scarce good, flushes in the shadows.
And it is not his; it is the face of the murderer on the paper, the
    villain,
the florist, or the circumstantial soccer hero.

ACKNOWLEDGMENT

JORGE AULICINO would like to thank Judith Filc for translation of this book.

OTHER BOOKS FROM TUPELO PRESS

Silver Road (memoir), Kazim Ali
Another English: Anglophone Poems from Around the World (anthology),
    edited by Catherine Barnett and Tiphanie Yanique
gentlessness (poems), Dan Beachy-Quick
Personal Science (poems), Lillian-Yvonne Bertram
Brownwood (poems), Lawrence Bridges
Everything Broken Up Dances (poems), James Byrne
One Hundred Hungers (poems), Lauren Camp
Almost Human (poems), Thomas Centolella
Rapture & the Big Bam (poems), Matt Donovan
Hallowed: New and Selected Poems (poetry), Patricia Fargnoli
Poverty Creek Journal (memoir), Thomas Gardner
Leprosarium (poems), Lise Goett
Other Fugitives and Other Strangers (poems), Rigoberto González
My Immaculate Assassin (novel), David Huddle
A God in the House: Poets Talk About Faith (interviews), edited by Ilya
    Kaminsky and Katherine Towler
A Camouflage of Specimens and Garments (poems), Jennifer Militello
The Cowherd's Son (poems), Rajiv Mohabir
Marvels of the Invisible (poems), Jenny Molberg
Yes Thorn (poems), Amy Munson
Lucky Fish (poems), Aimee Nezhukumatathil
The Life Beside This One (poems), Lawrence Raab
Intimate: An American Family Photo Album (hybrid memoir), Paisley
    Rekdal
The Voice of That Singing (poems), Juliet Rodeman
Walking Backwards (poems), Lee Sharkey
Good Bones (poems), Maggie Smith
Babel's Moon (poems), Brandon Som
Service (poems), Grant Souders
Swallowing the Sea (essays), Lee Upton
Butch Geography (poems), Stacey Waite

See our complete list at www.tupelopress.org